DOLORES
HUERTA
LABOR LEADER AND CIVIL RIGHTS ACTIVIST

SPECIAL LIVES IN HISTORY THAT BECOME

Signature LIVES

DOLORES
HUERTA

LABOR LEADER AND CIVIL RIGHTS ACTIVIST

by Robin S. Doak

Content Adviser: Sujay Rao, Ph.D.,
Department of History,
Gustavus Adolphus College

Reading Adviser: Rosemary G. Palmer, Ph.D.,
Department of Literacy, College of Education,
Boise State University

Compass Point Books ✦ Minneapolis, Minnesota

Compass Point Books
3109 West 50th Street, #115
Minneapolis, MN 55410

Editor: Anthony Wacholtz
Page Production: Bobbie Nuytten
Photo Researcher: Svetlana Zhurkin
Cartographer: XNR Productions, Inc.
Library Consultant: Kathleen Baxter

Creative Director: Keith Griffin
Editorial Director: Nick Healy
Managing Editor: Catherine Neitge

Library of Congress Cataloging-in-Publication Data
Doak, Robin S. (Robin Santos), 1963
  Dolores Huerta : labor leader and civil rights activist / by Robin S. Doak.
          p. cm.—(Signature lives)
Includes bibliographical references and index.
ISBN 978-0-7565-3477-6 (library binding)
1. Huerta, Dolores, 1930- —Juvenile literature. 2. Women labor Leaders—
United States—Biography—Juvenile literature. 3. Mexican American
migrant agricultural laborers—Biography—Juvenile literature. 4. Migrant
agricultural laborers—Labor unions—United States—History—Juvenile
literature. 5. United Farm Workers—History—Juvenile literature.
I. Title. II. Series.
HD6509.H84D63 2008
331.4'7813092—dc22   2007032696

Visit Compass Point Books on the Internet at *www.compasspointbooks.com*
or e-mail your request to *custserv@compasspointbooks.com*

Signature Lives

MODERN AMERICA

Life in the United States since the late 19th century has undergone incredible changes. Advancements in technology and in society itself have transformed the lives of Americans. As they adjusted to this modern era, people cast aside old ways and embraced new ideas. The once silenced members of society—women, minorities, and young people—made their voices heard. Modern Americans survived wars, economic depression, protests, and scandals to emerge strong and ready to face whatever the future holds.

Dolores Huerta

Table of Contents

1 IT CAN BE DONE

❦

On Easter Sunday in 1966, about 10,000 marchers and onlookers gathered around California's Capitol in Sacramento. Many of the marchers, most of them male farmworkers, had walked almost 300 miles (480 kilometers) from Delano, a farming community in south-central California, to the capital.

In the sea of male faces, one woman stood out. Standing next to the march organizer, Cesar Chavez, on the Capitol steps was a small, dark-haired woman dressed in red and black. Dolores Huerta may not have seemed like a force for change at first glance. What could this woman know about farmworkers' troubles? How could she make a difference?

Those who knew Dolores Huerta knew better. They had seen the fire and passion in her eyes when

Dolores Huerta spent much of her life fighting for the rights of others.

she talked about the problems facing U.S. farmworkers. Four years earlier, Huerta had helped Chavez found the National Farmworkers Association (NFWA). The NFWA was one of the first unions in the nation to fight for the rights of farmworkers.

Even before she met Chavez, Huerta was a force for the rights of Chicanos—people of Mexican descent. As a member of the Community Service

Chavez showed support for the gathered crowd of strikers and supporters in Sacramento.

Organization (CSO), Huerta persuaded lawmakers in California to think about the less fortunate throughout the state.

Although Chavez was the face of the union, Huerta was the union's hands and heart. She received most of the publicity during the strike and the boycott that followed. Working behind the scenes, she organized picket lines and boycotts. She traveled around the state persuading groups to support the union. She negotiated with growers for better working conditions.

Those who knew Huerta knew she never backed down. She was fearless and passionate, and she worked tirelessly to make the world a better and fairer place.

Years after the gathering in Sacramento, a union organizer said of her:

> *The wonder of Dolores Huerta is that she has never given up struggling for what is right, decent and human in the world, and she never will.*

Now, with all eyes upon her on the Capitol steps, Huerta began to speak. She scolded California Governor Edmund G. Brown for not appearing at the gathering. She warned other politicians, "We will be counted as your supporters only when we can count you among ours."

Thousands of people gathered at the California Capitol on April 11, 1966, to support an ongoing grape boycott.

She continued to speak out against injustice and inequality, stating:

> *The workers are on the rise. There will be strikes all over the state, and throughout the nation ... the workers know now, they are no longer alone.*

She told the workers that the sun was about to shine.

Those who heard Huerta that day learned that her voice was strong.

For four decades, Huerta would continue her work to improve conditions for farmworkers. She was arrested more than 20 times, beaten by police, and separated from her children for long stretches. But she never backed down, and she never gave up. When others told her that something would not work, Huerta disagreed. She lived by her favorite saying: *Sí, se puede*, which means, "Yes, it can be done."

As the most visible female leader in the United Farm Workers (UFW) union, Huerta set an example for other Chicanas and other women across the nation. She gave women a voice in the labor movement and showed them that one woman can be an effective force for change.

One of the first important farmworkers unions in the United States was the Japanese-Mexican Labor Association. Formed in 1903, the union was made up of sugar beet workers in California. This marked one of the first times that workers from two minority groups joined to gain better working conditions. Union officials organized a successful strike in Oxnard, California. However, the group fell apart soon after the strike ended.

2 LEARNING ABOUT RACISM

❦

Dolores Clara Fernández was born April 10, 1930, in Dawson, a small coal-mining town in northern New Mexico. Dolores' father, Juan Fernández, was the son of Mexican immigrants. His parents had migrated to the United States shortly before Juan was born. Juan worked as a coal miner in Dawson. He earned extra money as a migrant farmworker, traveling from state to state in the Southwest picking vegetables. Dolores' mother was Alicia Chavez Fernández.

When Dolores was 3 years old, her parents divorced. Dolores and her two siblings—an older brother, John, and a younger brother, Marshall—moved to Stockton, California, with their mother.

Dolores' mother remarried and worked hard to support her family. During the day, she worked as

Through much of the 20th century, Mexican migrant workers had to endure hard labor day after day to support their families.

a waitress at a restaurant. At night, she worked in a Stockton cannery. She eventually saved enough money to buy a restaurant and a 60-room hotel.

While Dolores' mother worked, her grandfather, Herculano Chavez, took care of Dolores, her brothers, and two new sisters. Dolores had a special bond with her grandfather, who had been disabled in a mining accident. He called her "seven tongues" because she liked to talk so much.

Dolores stayed in touch with her father. In 1938,

Stockton is a large city in the Central Valley, an agricultural area in the center of California.

Juan Fernández was elected to New Mexico's House of Representatives. As a politician, Fernández supported laws to protect workers. He served in the Navy during the Korean War and later earned a college degree. Dolores admired her father's ambition and hard work.

In Stockton, Dolores grew up in a neighborhood with people of many racial and cultural backgrounds. Mexicans, whites, blacks, and Asians all made their homes near her mother's hotel in Stockton. Fernández taught her children a valuable lesson by treating all of the neighbors equally and with respect. She also taught her children compassion by allowing poor farmworkers and their families to stay at the hotel for free.

> *Dolores grew up during the Great Depression, a time of economic hardship in the United States. The Depression also marked an increase in racism against Mexican-Americans in the country, especially in the Southwest. At a time when jobs were hard to find, many Americans blamed immigrants from Mexico and other nations for taking their jobs.*

Dolores' mother made sure that her children were exposed to the arts. She bought tickets for them to attend the symphony and go to the theater. She also signed Dolores up for piano, violin, and dance lessons. Dolores loved dancing, and she dreamed of being a flamenco dancer when she grew up.

Dolores was an active and happy child. She joined a church choir and became a Girl Scout. Her troop, made up of girls from diverse backgrounds, focused on citizenship within the Stockton community. During World War II, the girls raised money to help the United Service Organizations (USO) entertain U.S. troops overseas.

As they got older, Dolores and her siblings helped their mother by working in the hotel. They learned how to clean rooms, work at the front desk, and do other tasks. Dolores later remembered that her

Streetcars ran down Main Street in Stockton.

mother treated her and her two brothers the same. She said:

> *At home, we all shared equally in the household tasks. I never had to cook for my brothers or do their clothes like many traditional Mexican families. ... There was no idea that men were superior.*

When Dolores entered Stockton High School, she was a popular, outspoken student who believed that all people should be treated fairly. She soon learned that not everyone felt the same way. In high school, Dolores realized for the first time that her family was poor compared with many of the other students' families. She also learned that, as a person of Mexican descent, she was treated differently from white students.

One of Dolores' first experiences with racism came after she placed second in a national Girl Scout essay contest. Her prize was a trip to the Hopi Indian Reservation in Gallup, New Mexico. She received permission from her teachers to miss school to go on the trip. However, a school official refused to let her take the time off. Dolores believed that the

To make sure her children remained proud of their ancestry, Dolores' mother took them to Mexico City when Dolores was 17. Dolores later said, "This trip opened my eyes to the fact that there was nothing wrong with Chicanos."

official discriminated against her because she was of Mexican descent. She knew that white girls who had won the contest in the past had been allowed to miss classes to visit the reservation.

As a senior, Dolores was upset when she received a final grade of C in her English course. She had worked hard all year, earning A's on her essays and reports. The teacher told Dolores that someone else must have written her papers, because she did not believe Dolores could write them herself. Dolores remembered:

> *That really discouraged me because I used to stay up all night and think, and try to make every paper different, and try to put words in there that I thought were nice.*

Dolores soon realized that racism was not confined to her high school. She and her friends started a youth club in an empty storefront. There, kids of all races and backgrounds gathered to play ping-pong, dance, and talk. The club was soon shut down by local police. "They told us they didn't want to see all those white kids playing around with all these … Mexicans," Dolores remembered.

She also learned that racism could be violent and dangerous. Soon after World War II ended, Stockton youths wanted to celebrate. Dolores' brother Marshall put on a zoot suit, the long tailored jacket and baggy

pants that some young Mexican-American men wore. Then he left the house to meet his friends. As Dolores and a friend walked to a dance, they found her brother slumped in a doorway. He had been badly beaten, and his new clothes were torn. Marshall had been attacked because his clothes had identified him as a Mexican-American.

Dolores' brother was not the first victim. In Los Angeles in June 1943, some Mexican-American youths wearing zoot suits were stripped of their clothes and beaten.

In June 1943, a series of fights in Los Angeles became known as the zoot suit riots. The fights began when sailors told police they had been attacked by young Mexicans wearing zoot suits. Although it is unclear which side started the fighting, groups of sailors, soldiers, and civilians roamed the streets, attacking Mexican-Americans and anyone who did not look white. The zoot suit riots ended after police began arresting sailors and soldiers caught fighting.

In 1947, Dolores graduated from high school. She enrolled in college but left in 1950 to marry her high school sweetheart, an Irish-American named Ralph Head. In the coming years, Dolores and Ralph had two daughters together, Celeste and Lori. The marriage did not last, though, and they divorced in 1953.

After her divorce, Dolores returned to college to study education at the University of the Pacific's Delta College and the College of the Pacific in Stockton. Dolores' mother was proud of her daughter, the first in the family to attend college. Fernández helped by taking care of her two small granddaughters while Dolores attended classes.

After Dolores left college, she began teaching elementary school in a poor, rural area. Many of her students were children of migrant farmworkers. Dolores quickly decided that she needed to do something more to help these needy children. "I couldn't stand seeing farm worker children come to class hungry and in need of shoes," she said. "I thought I could do more by organizing their parents

The College of the Pacific in Stockton offered night classes that Dolores was able to work into her schedule.

than by trying to teach their hungry children."

After a year of teaching, Dolores decided to find a career that would allow her to do more for farmworkers and their families. Although worried about how she would make ends meet, she quit her teaching job. The next morning, she found a box of groceries someone had left on her porch. To Dolores, it seemed to be a sign she was choosing the right path in life.

3 Choosing a New Path

After she left teaching, Dolores began looking for a way to help farmworkers and their families. In 1955, she was introduced to a man named Fred Ross at the Community Service Organization. The organization was a California group that Ross had formed to improve the lives of Mexican-Americans throughout the state.

Since its founding in 1947, the CSO had been successful in improving Mexican-American communities. The group had pushed for new medical clinics and streetlights to make neighborhoods safer. Ross and his workers helped get a Mexican-American elected to Los Angeles' city council. They also worked to have more Spanish-speaking people hired in hospitals, police departments, and other government offices.

Fred Ross (front, center) and the other CSO members worked to advance the Mexican-American community.

Dolores was introduced to Ross by the Reverend Thomas McCullough, the priest at her Roman Catholic church. McCullough felt that the fiery, determined Dolores would be perfect for the activist organization. Once she agreed to work with the CSO, Dolores began organizing a drive to register people—especially minorities—to vote. She later founded a CSO branch in her hometown of Stockton.

While working at the CSO, Dolores met and married Ventura Huerta. During their marriage, the two had five children together: Fidel, Emilio, Vincent, Alicia, and Angela. Dolores remembered:

> *All the Huerta kids were born during the big CSO fights. I was always pregnant. I don't remember anything about Alicia's childhood except nursing her in the ladies' room during breaks in city council meetings or dropping her off at a friend's house.*

In 1957, she was introduced to a co-worker named Cesar Chavez, a quiet, unassuming man who was well-known within the Chicano community. Ross often spoke highly of him. Huerta said:

> *Fred kept talking about Cesar this and Cesar that. … I was very unimpressed. Fred had talked so much about this great organizer, and I found Cesar was very*

*shy. The first two or three years I knew
him, it was difficult to have a conversa-
tion with him.*

Little did Huerta know that the two would soon forge
a strong partnership, one that allowed them to fight
for workers' rights for more than 30 years.

Chavez's early life was very different from
Huerta's. Chavez was born near Yuma, Arizona, in
1927. His parents lost their farm during the Great
Depression, and they moved to California to find
work in the vegetable fields and fruit orchards there.

*Cesar Chavez
shared a
passion with
Huerta for
improving
conditions for
farmworkers.*

Chavez and his family moved from one labor camp to another, picking whatever crop was ready for harvesting. Because of the frequent moves, Chavez attended more than 30 elementary schools and only completed the eighth grade.

After spending two years in the Navy, Chavez went back to work in the fields. In 1946, he took part in his first strike as a member of the National Farm Labor Union. Soon after, he started doing volunteer work in the union's office while he worked in the fields. He eventually met Ross and went to work at the CSO.

Like Huerta, Chavez was deeply concerned about farmworkers in the United States. For decades, farmworkers—most of them of Mexican ancestry—had labored under terrible conditions. Unprotected by federal labor laws, they were paid very low wages. There were no toilets in the fields, and workers sometimes had to pay for a drink of water.

Many lived in labor camps made up of tents or small shacks with dirt floors. Many camps had no running water or electricity. Like Chavez's family, farmworker families moved from place to place, following the harvesting schedule across the nation. Their children switched

> In a 1960 *documentary* called Harvest of Shame, *broadcaster* Edward R. Murrow *quoted a farmer talking about his migrant workers:* "We used to own our slaves. Now we just rent them."

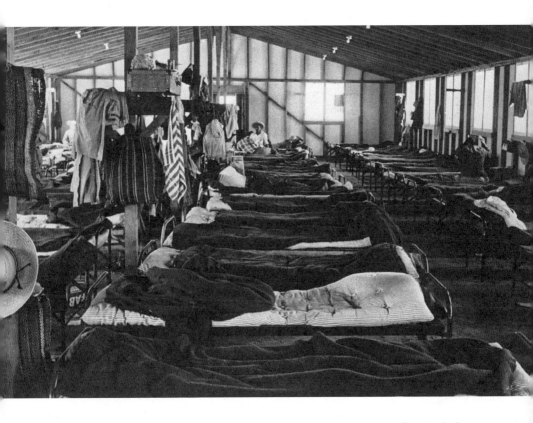

from school to school or worked in the fields along-side their parents.

How could growers treat their employees so poorly? Huerta explained:

In a typical labor camp, cots were packed closely together, and cleanliness and sanitation were constantly a problem.

> *Growers dehumanize their workers. ... Why would you refuse to give workers a toilet? Because if you don't give them a toilet, then they're not human beings. Why would you allow workers to be sprayed with pesticides? Growers view workers as tools.*

Mexican-American farmhands often spent many hours each day on their knees picking tomatoes and other vegetables.

In the late 1950s, Huerta decided to become more involved in the fight to help farmworkers.

> *Farmworkers work very hard. They pick tons of fruits and vegetables—not pounds, tons—every day to feed the nation. ... The people who feed us should earn enough so that they can nourish their own bodies. Growers live all year from a seasonal harvest. Farmworkers should be able to as well.*

Huerta knew that the workers needed a union. "Workers who have a union contract aren't abused, yelled at, or treated like animals," she said. Huerta knew that without a union, the workers would continue to be abused by the growers.

In 1958, Huerta helped found the Agricultural Workers Association (AWA), a union for farmworkers. The following year, the AWA became part of a larger union, the Agricultural Workers Organizing Committee (AWOC). The AWOC itself was part of a large group of labor unions known as the American Federation of Labor-Congress of Industrial Organizations (AFL-CIO).

In her new role as a union organizer, Huerta was exposed to sexism for the first time. When she moved into a leadership role, many people were not happy. Some farmworkers refused to meet with her. Later, when she was Chavez's second-in-command, farmworkers would leave a meeting when they saw that Huerta would be running it.

Even those who worked most closely with her treated her differently. One of the priests involved in

One of the first female labor activists was Mary Harris Jones (1830–1930), better known as Mother Jones. Jones was an Irish immigrant who grew up in Canada. She migrated to the United States when she was a young woman. During the late 1800s and early 1900s, Jones fought for the rights of miners and other laborers in the United States. She helped miners set up labor unions and worked to end child labor.

the union told Huerta to go home and take care of her family. Huerta's mother overheard this comment. She told her daughter, "Do not listen to him. You are the one who has organized this, and you know what you're doing."

With her efforts focused on the union, Huerta's home life suffered. Ventura Huerta wanted his wife to be a better wife and mother, but helping farmworkers was more important to her than cleaning and cooking. In 1963, the two divorced. Around the same time, her mother died of cancer. Huerta relied on her brother and other relatives and friends to help her care for her children.

Huerta threw herself into her work at the CSO. She had recently been put in charge of the group's efforts to stay in touch with state lawmakers. Huerta's new role required her to lobby, or try to persuade California lawmakers to pass laws to help Mexican-Americans and poor people. Each working day, Huerta drove 50 miles (80 km) from Stockton to Sacramento, the capital of California, and then back again.

Although she knew nothing about lobbying, Huerta quickly learned that she had a talent for it. The lawmakers responded to her passionate arguments on behalf of Mexican-Americans. Her hard work soon paid off, and lawmakers passed several bills she had supported. One bill required that voting ballots, driver's license tests, and other government

documents be printed in English and Spanish. Another bill allowed poor Mexicans living in the United States to receive financial help from the government. Her speaking abilities and blunt, open communication style would continue to serve her well. 🪶

Huerta made many trips to the California State Capitol in Sacramento.

4 FOUNDING A UNION FOR FARMWORKERS

Chapter

❧⳾❧

In 1958, Cesar Chavez had become the head of the CSO. One of his goals for the group was to form a union to support farmworkers and migrant laborers. He knew that he had a strong ally in Dolores Huerta. She had worked hard for the AWA, leaving only after she became convinced that the group was not moving in the right direction.

One day Chavez said to her, "You know, farmworkers are never going to have a union unless you and I start it." Huerta thought her friend was joking, and laughed. "He asked me if I would help him," she said. "When I saw he was serious, I felt honored. Cesar knew that a real farmworkers' union was my burning desire."

Other CSO members, however, did not want to focus their efforts on farmworkers' rights. In 1961,

During her lobbying efforts, Huerta proudly displayed the symbolic eagle that represented the National Farm Workers Association.

the group voted against founding a farmworkers' union. Chavez immediately resigned. He and
his family moved to Delano, an agricultural city in
south-central California, to concentrate on founding
a union.

Right from the start, both Chavez and Huerta
agreed that the union would use nonviolent confron-
tation to improve the conditions of farmworkers in
California. Chavez had read about the teachings and
beliefs of Mohandas Gandhi, a man who fought for
India's independence from Great Britain for nearly 30
years. Gandhi believed that the best way to create
change was to disobey laws, but in a nonviolent
way. He led marches, protests, and demonstrations
in an effort to pressure the British government into
freeing India. He also fasted, or stopped eating food,
in an effort to publicize his fight against the British.
Gandhi's methods became known as "civil disobe-
dience" and were later used by Martin Luther King
Jr. and other civil rights leaders in the United States
during the 1950s and 1960s.

One of Huerta's first tasks was to find members for
the union. She and her children traveled throughout
the northern Central Valley, knocking on doors and
talking to farmworkers and their families. Her children helped by handing out leaflets with union information. Sometimes the Huerta family slept in their
car or on the ground. Sometimes she would wake

Mohandas Gandhi (1869–1948) was an inspiration for the nonviolent approach Huerta and Chavez adopted.

her children in the middle of the night to travel to another farm. Eventually they had enough members to have their first official convention.

The first meeting of the new union was held in September 1962. Nearly 300 people attended. They voted for officers, and Huerta was elected vice president. Members decided to call the union the National Farm Workers Association (NFWA).

Huerta and Chavez (right) were among the first officials of the NFWA.

At first, Huerta tried to balance her role in the union with her job at the CSO. She badly needed the CSO job to support her family. But eventually Chavez told her:

> *You have to leave your job. You can't work for a living and fight. You've got to do one or the other. … You take your choice.*

When Huerta asked him how she and her children would eat, Chavez said, "I don't know. We'll eat something."

In late 1962, Huerta resigned from the CSO, but she and her children remained in Stockton. From there, she traveled to farming communities in the area, trying to persuade workers to join the union. She also continued her lobbying efforts. Unlike Chavez, Huerta believed that important changes could be made by talking to lawmakers. When Chavez visited the state capital in December 1962, Huerta's efforts were obvious. He said, "Everyone knows her, and the usual remark is that she is a fighter."

In 1964, at the end of the school year, Huerta moved to Delano. She and Chavez agreed that they needed to focus their efforts on the Imperial Valley area. At first Huerta and six of her children moved in with Chavez, his wife Helen, and their eight children. Eventually she saved enough money to move into her own home.

Although Chavez was the union's leader, he was always quick to tell people that he and Huerta were

> *At the first NFWA meeting, Chavez's brother Richard introduced his design for the union's flag. The flag had a bright red background. In the center was a large black eagle centered in a white circle. At the meeting, Richard Chavez said, "When that ... bird flies the problems of the farm workers will be solved." From this point on, Huerta would often wear black and red, the colors of the union.*

the two "architects" of the group. In turn, Huerta did not resent Chavez's public role. She remembered something that her mother had once told her:

> *When you see something that needs to be done, especially someone [who] needs help, you have to help them. And don't expect any compensation or reward for what you've done because what you're doing is a reward in itself.*

The union started slowly. Chavez was unsure whether the NFWA would be able to challenge the powerful growers. The growers had more money and more support from local and state lawmakers and police.

At first, Chavez, his wife Helen, his cousin Manuel Chavez, and Huerta—the group's core organizers—worked in the union office, which was in the Chavez family's home. Chavez wrote letters and newsletters to promote the union, and Helen Chavez was the union's bookkeeper. Huerta and Manuel Chavez worked to increase the union's membership.

Huerta and Manuel Chavez labored side-by-side with other farmworkers picking grapes. While they picked, they talked to the workers about the union and how it could help them. The money they earned also helped finance the new union.

The organizers also spread the word by holding "house meetings." They met with groups of workers

Huerta (right) worked beside many of the farmworkers, using the time as an opportunity to discuss the union.

in the safety of a worker's home to talk about joining the union. This was much safer than meeting in a public place. Growers often fired workers on the spot if they were seen talking to union organizers. Huerta explained:

> *When you go to a company without a union contract, the workers are afraid to talk. They're afraid to even look at you. Workers without a union feel helpless. ... They need their jobs and they know that there are always more workers waiting*

to take their place. ... If workers ask questions—boom—they get fired. Growers fight tooth and nail to keep the workers from organizing because a union is the only way farmworkers can improve their situation.

Huerta assisted farmworkers who wanted to join the union by answering their questions and helping them fill out paperwork.

When she talked to workers, Huerta explained how being part of the union could protect them from the growers. She also tried to involve the workers in running the union. Both Huerta and Chavez believed

that the NFWA should be led and directed by the workers themselves. In time, farmworkers would serve in union field offices and work in the union's radio stations.

Huerta made sure that women were included in the labor movement. She knew that women would work hard and bring a different perspective to labor negotiations. She also knew that growers would be less likely to use violence against women on the picket line. Before long, nearly half of the NFWA organizers were women, something that was unheard of in other labor unions.

Two years after the NFWA was founded, the union had about 1,000 members. The number marked a milestone for Huerta and Chavez. The two now began collecting a $50 paycheck from the union every week. ✥

5 EARLY STRUGGLES

❧❦❧

In early 1965, the NFWA organized its first small strike. That year, workers at Mount Arbor, California's largest rose grower, came to the union for help. The workers had been promised $9 for every thousand plants, but they were only being paid about $6.50. The rose grower then sold the bushes for $350 per thousand.

Working in the rose arbors was not easy. Rose workers crawled on their knees all day long, slitting mature rosebushes and inserting buds into them as fast as possible in a process called grafting. If the job was not done correctly, the buds would not grow and the bush was worthless. Even experienced grafters suffered hundreds of cuts from the thorns on the rosebushes. Over time, the cuts caused the workers' fingers to turn black.

Huerta encountered many growers who became angry with her and were unwilling to negotiate.

Growing roses is still one of the most important horticultural industries in California.

In May, Dolores Huerta and Cesar Chavez helped 85 workers organize a strike against Mount Arbor. The strikers demanded higher wages. They also wanted to have a union represent them when dealing with the company. Although the workers voted to go on strike, they did not want to form a picket line at Mount Arbor.

Early in the strike, Huerta showed that she would do everything possible to make sure the strike succeeded. Chavez remembered:

We sent out ten cars to check on the people's homes. We found lights in five or six homes and knocked on the doors. ... We'd say, "Well, you're not going to work, are you?" And they'd say no. Dolores Huerta ... saw a light in one house where four workers lived. They told her they were going to work, even after she reminded them of their pledge. So she moved the truck so that it blocked the driveway, turned off the key, put it in her purse and sat there alone.

One of Huerta's chief tasks as the union's vice president was to work out contracts between growers and workers. Shortly after the rose strike began, Chavez sent her to negotiate with the management. However, the company foreman was furious. While Huerta tried to reason with him, the foreman screamed at Huerta, calling her a communist. Although she stood firm

During the rose strike, Mount Arbor brought in replacement workers from a small town in Mexico. Cesar Chavez sent an angry letter to the Mexican town's mayor. Chavez said, "In those little Mexican towns, they have an old building where people go to read the news. On one side they list things like stray animals and on the other they have a list of criminals." The mayor posted Chavez's letter. He wanted the citizens of his town to know he thought the replacement workers were little better than criminals. In the coming years, most of the workers from this small Mexican town would join the union.

and tried to negotiate, the foreman called the police to have her removed.

The strike was not completely successful. After a week, the company agreed to give its workers a pay raise. However, no union contract had been signed with the NFWA. The rose workers had no protection against future problems.

While Huerta was working on the strike, her regard for Chavez grew. Although her personality was very different from his, she soon learned to respect his method of quiet leadership and fairness. Huerta knew he was as committed to the fight for workers' rights as she was, and he was just as willing to make sacrifices. Later she would call him a genius. Chavez also admired Huerta's gifts. He once said, "Dolores is absolutely fearless, physically and emotionally."

Although Huerta respected Chavez, she was not afraid to stand up to him. Their arguments began soon after she moved to Delano. "The people working under Cesar were overwhelmed by him," Huerta later said. "They found it hard to make a decision, or they wouldn't fight with him. When I think he's wrong, or when I think my way is

Although Chavez said she was fearless, Huerta admitted that there were many times when she was nervous and fearful. Years later, she said, "One thing I've learned … is that having tremendous fears and anxieties is normal. … By doing whatever causes your anxiety you overcome the fear, and strengthen your emotional, spiritual, activist muscles."

better, I fight with him." She explained why Chavez was so quick to argue with her: "He knows I'll never quit so he uses me to let off steam; he knows I'll fight back anyway."

After the rose strike, Huerta and Chavez turned their attention to California's grape workers. These workers earned about 90 cents an hour, plus an extra 10 cents for every big basket they filled with

Migrant workers had to cut the grapes off the vine quickly to meet the quota of the growers. They also had to be precise so the grapes would not be damaged.

grapes. In addition to low pay, the conditions in the fields were appalling. Many growers ignored the state's standards for worker safety, refusing to supply toilets and charging workers for a cup of water on a hot day. Workers still lived in unheated, unsanitary shacks with their families. At this time, the average life expectancy for a farmworker was 49 years.

The first hints of worker unrest began in the Coachella Valley in southern California. Growers there had been given permission by the government to bring in workers from Mexico to work the grape harvest. However, the growers had to abide by two conditions: The guest workers were to be paid $1.25 an hour, and they could never be paid more than U.S. workers. The growers responded by cutting the wages of U.S. workers, which in turn meant that the guest workers could also be paid less.

U.S. workers, many of Philippine ancestry, were enraged at the wage cut. Led by Larry Itliong, a Filipino labor activist and Agricultural Workers Organizing Committee (AWOC) organizer, they walked out of the fields and went on strike. After less than two weeks, the growers struck a bargain with the strikers. Worried that their grapes would rot on the vines, they agreed to pay everyone $1.25 per hour. However, they would not sign a contract with a union.

A Filipino worker supported the AWOC during a strike.

In late summer, many of the same workers who had gone on strike in the Coachella Valley moved north to Delano to work the grape harvest there. Encouraged by their earlier success, they again asked for $1.25 per hour and the right to form a union. The

> Workers who are brought in to break strikes are often called "scabs" by strikers. Noted author Jack London offered a more colorful definition of a scab: "After God had finished the rattlesnake, the toad, and the vampire, He had some awful substance left with which He made a scab. A scab is a two-legged animal with a corkscrew soul, a water-logged brain, a combination backbone made of jelly and glue. ... The modern strikebreaker sells his birthright, his country, his wife, his children, and his fellow men for an unfilled promise from his employer, trust or corporation."

growers agreed to pay the workers the wage they wanted, but they refused to allow a union to come in. The workers responded by going on strike.

The growers in Delano were not prepared to give in. After the strike had gone on for five days, the growers hired Mexican-American workers to replace the striking Filipinos. They also evicted striking workers from the company-owned camps where they lived.

In the late 1950s, Itliong had helped Huerta organize the AWA. Now he was leading the strike in Delano. Huerta visited Itliong on the picket lines, talking to him and the strikers, then reporting back to Chavez. Both Huerta and Itliong believed that the NFWA members should join the Filipino strikers on the picket lines. Chavez was more reluctant. The NFWA was still a new group with just $80 in its bank account.

At this time, Huerta had seven children to take care of. The Chavezes had eight. But when the union officials met to discuss supporting the AWOC strike,

Larry Itliong (1942–1976) and the AWOC joined forces with the NFWA to gain support for the strike.

Helen Chavez said, "Well, we have to support the strike!" On September 16, Mexico's Independence Day, NFWA members met at a church in Delano. There they voted to join the Filipino workers on the picket lines. Little did Huerta know that the union would be on strike for the next five years. ☙

6 LA HUELGA

Chapter

❧⟨⟩☙

Days after the NFWA voted to strike, union members began manning the picket lines beside the Filipino farmworkers. The NFWA had grown since its founding and had more members than the AWOC. Chavez, Huerta, and other NFWA officials quickly took a leading role in the strike. By the end of September, several thousand workers—mostly Chicano—were striking on 30 farms.

Because these farms were located many miles apart, the union set up "roving pickets." Each day, picketers showed up at different fields, traveling together in cars and vans. Union workers watched each farm to see whether the grower was bringing in strikebreakers to replace the striking workers. If a farm used strikebreakers, a union worker would

Dolores Huerta spent much of her time organizing the grape pickers' strike.

radio this information to headquarters in Delano. Officials would then dispatch picketers to the farm.

At the farms, union workers tried to talk to the strikebreakers. They wanted the replacement workers to understand what the union was fighting for and why it was important to respect the picket line. As a result, many strikebreakers walked out of the fields and joined the strike—and the NFWA.

Growers tried various methods to end the strike. They went to court and got an order that banned picketing. They also got an order preventing workers from wearing shirts that said *huelga*, or "strike."

Sometimes the growers resorted to violence. One large grower sprayed picketing workers with pesticides, harmful chemicals used to destroy insects, fungi, or other pests that could harm crops. Picketers were sometimes beaten or sprayed with pepper spray. Their cars were even run off the roads by tractors and other vehicles.

Huerta learned about the violence firsthand. One day she and a group of picketers were driving back from the fields. Their car overheated, and they walked to a nearby house for water. The picketers were greeted at the front door by a grower holding a shotgun. He fired the weapon over their heads and ordered them to leave.

Instead of the growers and their supporters being arrested, however, strikers were usually the ones

taken to jail. During the course of the strike, hundreds of union members were arrested. Throughout her life, Huerta was arrested more than 20 times.

Delano officials and police officers also harassed

union organizers, members, and sympathizers. City inspectors were sent to the union headquarters to make trouble, and the police followed the cars of people who visited the union. Soon after the strike began, someone fired bullets into empty cars parked in front of union headquarters.

The strike, which became known as *La Huelga*, lasted five years. During this time, the union continued to follow a policy of nonviolence. No matter how badly the growers and others treated union members, they continued to peacefully protest for their rights. Their commitment to nonviolence attracted many supporters.

Chavez traveled throughout the region to raise awareness about the strike and the fight for Latino rights, known as *La Causa*. When he visited colleges, he often asked students to donate money to support the workers, especially those who had been arrested. In one day, Chavez raised almost $7,000.

To spread the word, strike supporters traveled to California cities to speak. Many had to hitchhike because they had no money for gas. They visited church groups and community organizations. Their hard work paid off, and soon money, clothes, and food were being sent from California and other states to aid the unemployed strikers. Others traveled to Delano to take part in the picketing.

The timing of the strike fit perfectly with the push

for civil rights throughout the nation. During the 1950s and 1960s, African-Americans in the South and other parts of the nation used nonviolence to fight for fair and equal treatment. Lunch-counter sit-ins, Freedom Rides, and a massive civil rights march in Washington, D.C., all helped publicize segregation and discrimination in the United States. Americans were more likely than ever before to pay attention to the problems faced by other groups, including farmworkers.

Chavez also tried some of the tactics that the civil rights workers in the South had used. In early 1966, he began planning a roughly 300-mile (480-km) march from Delano to Sacramento to protest against

Chavez explained his idea for a long-distance march to a crowd of excited migrant workers as Huerta (right) looked on.

the grape growers. The march, which Chavez called a pilgrimage, was inspired by a similar one in 1965. That year, civil rights activists marched from Selma, Alabama, to Montgomery, the state's capital, for voting rights.

Grape pickers and supporters carried the American flag and NFWA banner as they marched from Delano to Sacramento.

The farmworkers' march began when Chavez and 70 other strikers set off for the capital on March 17, 1966. Huerta and most of the other women remained behind to keep the picket lines going strong.

As Chavez and the workers marched, hundreds

of people joined them. They held rallies every day to support workers' rights. Every night, the union's theatrical troupe, *El Teatro Campesino*, performed for the marchers. On the back of a flatbed truck, the actors put on plays about the farmworkers' struggles.

By the time the marchers arrived in Sacramento, 10,000 people had joined Chavez. Although Governor Brown had left town, Huerta was waiting at the capital. She brought good news with her. She had negotiated a contract with one of the largest grape growers in the region. It was the union's first victory.

After the march to Sacramento, Martin Luther King Jr. sent a telegram to the union:

> As brothers in the fight for equality, I extend the hand of fellowship and good will and wish continuing success to you and your members. The fight for equality must be fought on many fronts—in the urban slums,

In 1965, playwright Luis Valdez founded El Teatro Campesino, or the "Farmworkers Theater." Valdez, a former farmworker himself, founded the theater company to raise money to support the farmworkers' strike. The theater company used farmworkers as actors and the fields or backs of trucks as stages. The plays showed Valdez's pride in being Mexican. They also motivated Latino workers to fight for their civil rights. Valdez earned national attention as a playwright after his play Zoot Suit *made it to Broadway and Hollywood. He also wrote the screenplay for the 1987 movie* La Bamba *about 1950s pop star Ritchie Valens. Valdez's writing has earned him many awards and honors.*

in the sweat shops of the factories and fields. Our separate struggles are really one—a struggle for freedom, for dignity, for humanity. ... We are together with you in spirit and in determination that our dreams for a better tomorrow will be realized.

The union's march to Sacramento was inspired by similar marches of civil rights activists.

The march to Sacramento attracted national attention. The U.S. Senate decided to hold a hearing

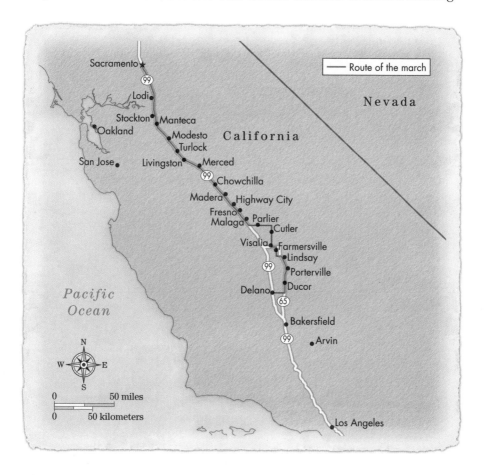

on the conditions in the farm fields of California. In fall of 1966, Senator Robert Kennedy and other members of the U.S. Senate Subcommittee on Migratory Labor arrived in Delano. As Kennedy listened to the testimony, he became angry over the way farmworkers were treated. He would prove a strong supporter for the union.

The year 1966 brought another change to the union. After the march, the NFWA merged with the AWOC to form the United Farm Workers Organizing Committee (UFWOC), a part of the AFL-CIO. Later the union would change its name to the United Farm Workers. Chavez was named the union's president. ℘

During the strike, Huerta was a familiar face in the fields and at union headquarters. Striking workers began calling her la Madre de la Huelga, or "the Mother of the Strike." She was also known as "Dolores Huelga." Her name, Dolores Huerta, translates into "Sorrow in the Fields."

7 A BOYCOTT BEGINS

℮∽✕∽℮

After moving to Delano, Dolores Huerta's family grew. She and Richard Chavez, Cesar's brother, had four children together: Juanita, María Elena, Ricky, and Camila. But the strike years were a time of hardship for the growing family, and they ate mainly tortillas and beans. Huerta remembered:

> *We were extremely poor, so poor that our clothes came from donations and second-hand clothing stores—in fact, second-hand-store clothes were a luxury for us. ... In the union we worked for five dollars a week at first, and later 10 dollars a week. ... All my children were raised in a lifestyle of extreme deprivation—they didn't have toys or clothes.*

Donning an NFWA poncho, Dolores Huerta spoke to a crowd of migrant workers during a rally.

Susan Samuels Drake, a reporter who worked with Huerta, recalled, "It's no secret that her 11 children often weren't sure where to get dinner or plop their heads on a pillow during the 60's, 70's and 80's." Although Huerta tried to take her children with her whenever possible, they often remained in Delano while she traveled. Her daughter Lori said, "She was always on the road, and we were left to take care of ourselves." Union volunteers babysat the Huerta children.

Huerta admitted that her activism took a toll on her children. The kids were often split among different households when she was gone, and Huerta sometimes missed their birthdays and holidays. Although they missed their mother, the children came to understand why Huerta had to go. Lori remembered:

> When I was going to turn 13, we had been in Delano for a year. My mother was going to Florida, to take on Coca Cola. I was upset; it was going to be my birthday. I was at the office and I said, "We don't even see you, my birthday is coming, why can't you be with me?" My mother said, "Your birthday is important, I

Sometimes Huerta's children used her own union tactics against her. One night Huerta allowed her boys to spend the night in an abandoned building that was rumored to be haunted, but she refused to allow the girls to go along. The girls made signs and surrounded Huerta's car in the driveway. They told her that she was sexist and unfair. Although Huerta was impressed by the picketing, the girls were still not allowed to go to the sleepover.

understand what you are saying. But you have to understand there are thousands and thousands of farm worker children out there who don't get to celebrate their birthdays. You can help me by sacrificing your birthday."

Lori always remembered her mother's words:

Giving kids clothes and food is one thing, you know, but it's much more important to teach them that other people besides themselves are important, and that the best thing they can do with their lives is to use them in the service of other people.

Keeping in mind Mexican-American parents who had to bring their children to the field with them to pick, Huerta taught her own children to be selfless.

Huerta sometimes recruited her children as mini-activists. In 1965, Huerta and her 9-year-old son Emilio were outside a workers' camp in El Paso, Texas. Union members wanted to get some leaflets into the camp, and Huerta asked her son whether he would take them in. He thought for a while, then said, "Okay, I'm ready." Huerta remembered:

> *We gave him this big stack of leaflets to take to the women inside the camp ... then we waited for him to come out. Pretty soon here comes Emilio just running as fast as his little legs would carry him, with [the camp's] personnel manager ... coming behind him in a car. The poor little boy! When he got to the edge of the road he just collapsed, out of breath. But he wasn't hurt or scared, so it was really funny. He had gotten the leaflets into the camp.*

Emilio, like many of Huerta's other children, would become involved in the fight for civil rights as an adult.

The events of 1966 had proved that the union could be successful. With national attention, it could get more growers to sign contracts that were good for farmworkers. Huerta, with the help of Fred Ross, began thinking about new ways to draw attention to the ongoing strike. In December 1967, the union announced plans for a nationwide boycott of

Chavez rallied a group of about 400 people for a grape boycott in Seattle, Washington.

grapes. Chavez and Huerta hoped that they could persuade grocery store owners and consumers to stop buying grapes.

In January 1968, Huerta, 40 farmworkers, and 10 student volunteers boarded the union's yellow school bus and traveled across the country to New York City. Huerta also took her children. The bus had no heater, and the travelers had to sleep in churches and other places along the way. By the time they arrived in New York, many people were sick.

In New York, Huerta organized pickets, rallies, and press conferences. She made sure that the news media were aware of these activities. With bullhorns blaring and union flags waving, the workers made sure that people in the city got the message. In interviews and other appearances, Huerta portrayed the growers as unreasonable and cruel.

People not associated with the union also supported the boycott on table grapes.

Huerta also worked to stop suppliers from sending grapes from California to market. She and some union members visited the Hunts Points

Terminal, the largest produce market in the nation. There they set up a picket line and tried to persuade buyers to support their boycott. They also picketed in front of grocery stores that would not support the boycott. Huerta and the UFW workers were joined on the picket line by members of church groups, students, and other citizens.

By the end of 1968, the sales of grapes were down by 20 percent in some major cities. As much as $4 million worth of grapes had rotted on the vines because there was no demand for them.

Huerta returned to California in 1969. She continued her work picketing and publicizing the boycott. She again persuaded small, independent grocers to join the effort. As a result, the boycott became more successful on the West Coast. ᔇ

8 NEGOTIATING A SETTLEMENT

Chapter

⌒⌒⌒

Dolores Huerta was one of the UFW's most effective chief negotiators. Those who knew her often described her as tough, passionate, and willing to fight. Huerta refused to back down or be intimidated by the growers and their lawyers. Negotiating with the growers was not easy. Huerta said:

> I speak heart-to-heart with the growers, but it doesn't do any good. ... I'm at the table with these guys and they're arrogant and bigoted. They think they're above the law. These guys have hearts of stone, literally. ... You have to force them into contracts. You have to make them better people by forcing them, just like in the South during the time of the civil rights struggle.

Huerta was a persistent and determined negotiator for the union.

Many of the growers dreaded working with Huerta. They called her the "dragon lady," as though she breathed fire when she spoke. One said, "Dolores Huerta is crazy. She's a violent woman,

Huerta's confidence in the union showed in her speeches.

where women, especially Mexican women, are usually peaceful and pleasant." Others complained that she was "too quick to attack, too slow to listen."

Growers also complained about Huerta's bringing workers to meetings with her. During negotiations, she would translate the growers' words into Spanish for the workers. "My speaking to workers in Spanish was to keep them apprised at all times of what was going on in the negotiations and to ask their opinion," she explained.

When the growers told Chavez they did not want to negotiate with Huerta, the union president defended her. He warned them that he was harder to deal with. Yet he also joked with union members about "unleashing" Huerta on the growers. Those who supported workers' rights had nothing but praise for Huerta and her methods. One California government worker said, "Huerta is a brave woman. She's a believer."

On *May* 10, 1969, International Boycott Day, the UFW released this statement: "*Mexicans, Filipinos, Africans and others, our ancestors were among those who founded this land and tamed its natural wilderness. ... If this road we chart leads to the rights and reforms we demand, if it leads to just wages, humane working conditions, protection from the misuse of pesticides, and to the fundamental right of collective bargaining, if it changes the social order that relegates us to the bottom reaches of society, then in our wake will follow thousands of American farm workers. Our example will make them free. ... For we are in the midst of a great social movement, and we will not stop struggling 'til we die, or win!"*

By 1970, the UFW claimed to have 50,000 dues-paying members. It had become the largest agricultural labor union in California history. As the strike moved into its fifth year, the union got closer to its first contract with a grape grower. On April 15, 1970, Freedman Ranches signed a contract with the UFW. Freedman was given a union label to put on its grapes to show consumers that the grapes were OK to purchase.

Three months later, as nonunion grapes rotted on store shelves, the union's hard work further paid off. On July 25, one of the largest growers agreed to sign a contract, which ended the strike. Huerta recalled:

> *It never, ever, ever, ever crossed my mind that it couldn't happen. Not once. I always knew that we would be able to do it.*

Four days later, Delano growers began coming to the union office to sign contracts with the UFW. By the end of 1970, the union had negotiated contracts with most of the grape growers in the area.

The new, three-year contracts were historic. Never before had the workers been guaranteed such rights. The contracts ensured higher wages and better health benefits. They instituted retirement plans and put a grievance procedure into place for workers who were fired. UFW members were also guaranteed

that they would be the first hired at the beginning of a new harvesting season. This allowed workers to settle down in one place. Their children could attend one school, and families could make connections in the community.

Chavez shook hands with a representative for table grape growers, marking the end of the boycott.

Huerta later reflected on why the strike was successful:

> *We took the fight from the fields to the cities. We took the fight from Delano to New York, Canada, and Europe. ... The vast majority of people don't like to see injustice. Farmworkers' poverty is so extreme and the growers are so wealthy. People look at the way farmworkers live, they see the things farmworkers don't have, and they ask, Why? Why aren't these workers paid fairly? It's not the consumers' fault. Consumers shouldn't feel bad, but they should be concerned. They should help ensure that the people who are feeding them are not exploited or abused.*

Although they had forced grape growers to come to terms with their workers, there was much more to be done.

Other farmworkers needed their help, and in the coming months Huerta and the UFW organized several more boycotts. They targeted California lettuce and wine grapes. These boycotts would continue until 1978.

With *La Huelga* at an end, Huerta returned to lobbying. She lived by her own motto, *Sí se puede*, or "Yes, it can be done." In 1971, she persuaded a California congressman to withdraw a bill that was weighted toward growers.

In 1973, she appeared before lawmakers and said:

My testimony ... is an appeal for justice for millions of men, women, and children who have been oppressed, mistreated, and exploited by their employers and their communities for many years.

Dolores Huerta appeared with Gayle Wilson, a lifelong children's advocate from California.

In 1975, California passed the Agricultural Labor Relations Act. The law was intended to "ensure peace in the agricultural fields by guaranteeing justice for all agricultural workers and stability in labor relations."

It was the first law to guarantee farmworkers the right to have a union to represent their interests. It also gave the workers the right to elect their own unions.

Over the years, the UFW has won many important rights for its members. These rights included breaks, toilets in the fields, clean drinking water, and places for workers to wash their hands.

The union also helped to get rid of the short-handled hoe. The hoe, only 2 feet (60 centimenters) long, forced workers to hunch over all day. It allowed farm overseers to quickly determine whether a farmworker was working.

Medical professionals blamed the hoe for causing back pain and more serious and permanent injuries. Known to the migrant workers as *el cortito*, or "the short one," the hoe caused the migrant workers to develop arthritis in the spine, as well as ruptured spinal disks. One worker challenged a grower:

> *Just stand up and hold the tips of your shoes and walk up and down this room and see how many times you can do it.*

Another worker referred to the hoe as "a flat-out symbol of oppression—a way to keep control of workers and make them live humbled, stooped-over lives." The hoe was banned in California in 1975. ℘

The short-handled hoe led to long-term back problems.

Chapter

9 CONTINUED ACTIVISM

❧⟨∞⟩❧

As a woman, Dolores Huerta had faced bias and discrimination that her male co-workers had not. Slowly Huerta became a feminist—someone who believes in equal rights for women and men. She was ready to fight for women's rights, and she encouraged other women to take part in strikes and boycotts.

"We are needed in public life because we think differently," she told them. "We have a different perspective." She also fought discrimination by pointing out biased remarks made by men in board rooms during business meetings. She said, "It was sort of an educational process for them … because they didn't realize."

In 1974, Huerta helped found the Coalition for Labor Union Women to encourage women to take leadership roles in unions. She has given speeches for

Dolores Huerta urged citizens to participate during a get-out-the-vote rally in downtown Los Angeles.

the National Organization for Women and served as a board member of the Feminist Majority Foundation. Both of these groups work for women's rights.

Huerta has also remained active in the drive for workers' rights and civil rights. In the mid-1980s, the UFW focused on the problem of pesticides. Farmworkers are exposed to pesticides when they handle the leaves of plants that have been sprayed.

A tractor equipped with a sprayer is used to apply pesticides to grape vines. The vines can be toxic when the plants touch a person's skin.

These pesticides can cause dizziness, vision problems, nausea, skin rashes, and breathing difficulties. They may also cause birth defects, illness, and even death.

Huerta worked hard to educate growers about the dangerous effects of pesticides. She said:

> *I personally know one family where the woman's husband got sick working in the strawberries in San Diego. He got on a bus and went home and died.*

To get growers to stop using pesticides, the union held another grape boycott, but this one was not successful. Chavez fasted to draw attention to the problem, and Huerta appeared before Congress to talk about the dangers of pesticides. Some lawmakers accused her of lying about the effects of the pesticide DDT.

George H.W. Bush

In 1988, Huerta appeared at a peaceful protest against Vice President George H.W. Bush in San Francisco. The protest was held in front

The first person to warn the world about the dangers of pesticides was author Rachel Carson. Her book Silent Spring *was* published in 1962. The book told people about the effects of pesticide pollution on the environment. Carson, a scientist, warned that some pesticides, especially DDT, could cause cancer or even kill animals and humans. The United States banned the use of DDT in 1972.

of a hotel where Bush was speaking. Huerta handed out leaflets and spoke to reporters, publicizing the grape boycott and campaigning against the Republican politician. But the peaceful protest turned into something far more serious.

As police tried to clear the sidewalk in front of the hotel, an officer badly beat Huerta with a baton. She was rushed by ambulance to a nearby hospital. Her son Emilio spoke to reporters outside the hospital, saying that the attack was not just a push or a beating over the head. With great detail, he explained that her spleen had been severely damaged from being stabbed.

Huerta suffered six broken ribs, and surgeons had to remove her spleen. The beating also affected her emotionally. For nearly a year and a half after the attack, the normally outgoing and fearless woman panicked in crowds.

Huerta knew that her activities put her at risk of injury. She said, "When you choose the path of the warrior, you can get beaten or shot at or even killed— that comes with the work." However, Huerta believed that the incident had made her a stronger person.

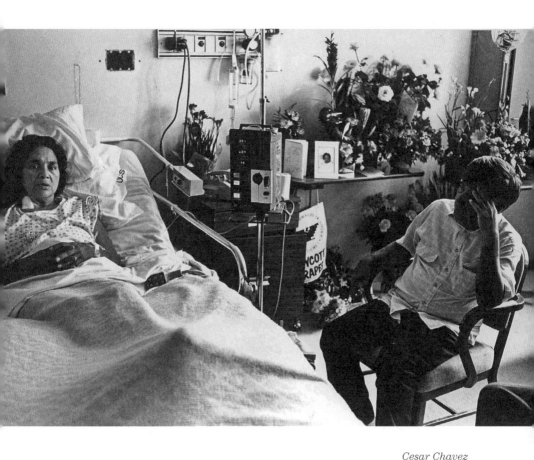

After Huerta recovered, she took time off from her work with the UFW to focus more on women's rights. She traveled around the nation, encouraging Latino and other women to run for elective office. She told women, "We want to go on and cut a path for our life, and we shouldn't let anyone stand in our way."

In April 1993, Huerta received word that her friend and union co-founder, Cesar Chavez, had died unexpectedly in Arizona. Chavez, who had been

Cesar Chavez visited Huerta at the hospital after the attack in San Francisco.

visiting a farm family on union business, died in his sleep from natural causes. Years of farm work and fasting had left him weak and unwell.

On April 29, Huerta and 35,000 other people traveled to Delano from across the nation to say goodbye to this man who had changed history. Carrying his simple wooden coffin, his friends, family, and admirers marched to Forty Acres, the UFW's field headquarters in Delano. Those closest to Chavez laid a carving of the UFW eagle and a short-handled hoe on his coffin. At the funeral, Huerta delivered the eulogy for her old friend. She said:

Thousands of mourners followed Chavez's casket to the funeral Mass.

> *Cesar died in peace ... with a serene look*
> *on his face. It was as if he had chosen to*

die at this time. ... He died so that we would wake up. He died so that the union might live.

After the funeral, Huerta went back to work for the union until a leader could be chosen to replace Chavez. Huerta felt it was her role to remind people that the work of the UFW must go on. She said:

We just don't want people to feel that hopes have been shattered because Cesar is gone. ... We know he is irreplaceable, but people have been trained to carry on the work of the union.

Arturo Rodriguez (1949–)

In 1994, a year after Chavez's death, Huerta took part in a march to commemorate her friend's life and legacy. The march was led by Arturo Rodriguez, the new UFW president and Chavez's son-in-law. Huerta and the others began the march in Delano and retraced the route of the 1966 march to Sacramento. When they arrived at the state Capitol,

In 1994, it was announced that Huerta would receive free ice cream for life from Ben & Jerry's for her years of activism for farmworkers and women. She and seven other social activists, including filmmaker Spike Lee and singer Carlos Santana, appeared in an advertisement for eight new ice cream flavors. A poster showing the eight advocates posing together was created, and profits from its sale were given to the Children's Defense Fund.

about 20,000 supporters were waiting to greet them.

In 2000, Huerta resigned from the UFW to focus on other activities. She was sidelined in October of that year, however, when doctors performed emergency surgery to repair a tear in her intestine. After the major operation, she spent weeks in the hospital, part of the time in the intensive-care unit. Doctors worried that Huerta might not survive.

Instead Huerta fought her way back to health and relearned how to walk, talk, and eat. The following year, she had recovered enough to lead a 165-mile (264-km) march from Bakersfield to Sacramento to persuade Governor Gray Davis to sign a bill that would help farmworkers. On September 30, 2002, Davis signed the bill. In a letter to Huerta, the governor told her that she was his conscience.

In 2002, Huerta received an award that let her pursue a lifelong dream. In December of that year, she was honored with the Nation/Puffin Award for Creative Citizenship. The award came with a $100,000 grant for her to use as she wished.

Huerta used the money to set up the Dolores Huerta Foundation in Bakersfield. The foundation trains people to be community activists and organizers. "Especially among new immigrants, we have

In 2002, Huerta and Rodriguez led a march from Bakersfield to the Capitol in Sacramento.

such a need for organization," Huerta explained. "The (foundation) is to show people that they're not helpless. They do have power." The group teaches people how to use CSO and UFW techniques, including house meetings and boycotts.

Even though Huerta's main focus is her foundation, she remains committed to the cause of farmworkers' rights. She recognizes that the union is still badly needed. In the late 1990s, Huerta recalled seeing something that angered her:

Huerta wants people to acknowledge the importance of all types of workers. She said, "We need to respect people who do things with their hands: farm workers, carpenters, mechanics. Just because you don't have a college degree it doesn't make you a lesser person. It takes courage to do what we want to do." She has told children of farmworkers to be proud of their family, proud of their heritage. She said, "Your parents and grandparents do the most sacred work in the world. They feed everybody."

> *I saw a woman in a tomato field during a school day. She had three of her kids out there with her and when she saw me she started apologizing. She said, "I had to take them out of school because we didn't have enough money to buy groceries." They're out there every single day, little kids picking tomatoes with their hands too small to even cover the ... tomato.*

Huerta wanted to get her point across in a strong way. She stated that workers are presented with a difficult question:

How can we survive? You go to their homes and see that they're barely making enough to feed and clothe their children. When I visit workers in their homes, I feel as if I'm back in the fifties when we started. People are still being exploited in the same way: little kids carrying twenty-five-pound buckets; twenty workers sharing a house just to pay rent.

Huerta realizes that things take time to change, and she refuses to give up.

In 2000, Huerta translated for Horacio Ortiz, a foreman who felt he was unjustly fired for refusing to order his crew to do an unreasonable amount of work.

Some of Huerta's awards include:

1984:
Outstanding Labor Leader Award from the California State Senate

1993:
National Women's Hall of Fame inductee

Roger Baldwin Medal of Liberty Award from the American Civil Liberties Union

Ellis Island Medal of Freedom Award

1998:
Woman of the Year honoree from Ms. magazine

100 Most Important Women of the 20th Century honoree from Ladies Home Journal

Eleanor Roosevelt Award for Human Rights

Looking ahead to the future, she said:

When you're young, you think that somehow things will get better and injustices will diminish. ... Now that I'm older, I see that the same injustices are still with us. Now I see the sons and daughters of the exploiters continue the same exploitation. In some cases things are even worse. ... That makes me sad, but I still believe that ... if we keep working and reaching out and educating people, then we can overcome. ... I've always had a lot [of] faith in people.

Over the years, many people have recognized Huerta's contributions to her favorite causes. Six schools have been named in her honor, and she has received seven honorary college degrees.

Activist, lobbyist, advocate, mother, wife, and grandmother—Dolores Huerta has played all of these roles and more. Thousands of farmworkers remember her as

the mother of the strike, the woman who said, "*Sí, se puede*," or "Yes, it can be done."

How would Dolores Huerta herself like to be remembered? "As a woman who cares for fellow humans," she has said. "We must use our lives to make the world a better place to live, not just to acquire things. That is what we are put on earth for." ༄

In 2000, Huerta joined more than 350 female speakers at a symposium in Baltimore, Maryland.

HUERTA'S LIFE

1930
Born in Dawson, New
Mexico

1947
Graduates from
Stockton High School

1950
Marries Ralph Head

1930

1932
The infant son of Anne
Morrow Lindbergh and
Charles Lindbergh is
kidnapped and murdered

1948
The modern nation
of Israel is founded

WORLD EVENTS

1957

Meets Cesar Chavez

1955

Begins working
for the Community
Service Organization;
marries Ventura
Huerta

1958

Co-founds the
Agricultural Workers
Association

1955

1955

Rosa Parks' refusal to give
up her seat on a bus to
a white man inspires the
civil rights movement

1959

Fidel Castro
becomes leader
of Cuba

1953

Sir Edmund Hillary of
New Zealand and Tenzing
Norgay of Nepal are the
first two men to reach the
summit of Mount Everest

HUERTA'S LIFE

1968
Travels to New York City to organize a boycott on the East Coast

1962
Co-founds the National Farmworkers Association

1964
Moves to Delano, California

1965

1966
The National Organization for Women (NOW) is established to work for equality between women and men

1963
Dr. Martin Luther King Jr. delivers his "I Have a Dream" speech to more than 250,000 people attending the March on Washington

1968
Civil rights leader Martin Luther King Jr. and presidential candidate Robert F. Kennedy are assassinated two months apart

WORLD EVENTS

1973

Testifies before
Congress about
conditions for
laborers on
U.S. farms

1974

Helps found the
Coalition for Labor
Union Women

1988

Hospitalized after
being beaten by a San
Francisco police officer
during a peaceful protest
against Vice President
George Bush

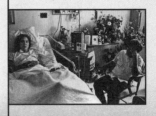

1975

1973

Spanish artist
Pablo Picasso
dies

1974

Scientists find that
chlorofluorocarbons—
chemicals in coolants
and propellants—are
damaging Earth's
ozone layer

1983

Sally Ride becomes the
first American woman
to travel in space

HUERTA'S LIFE

1994

Takes part in a commemorative march from Delano to Sacramento on the anniversary of Chavez's death

1993

Delivers the eulogy at the funeral of Cesar Chavez

1998

Receives the Eleanor Roosevelt Award for Human Rights

1990

1990

East and West Germany unite after 45 years of separation

1995

Astronaut Eileen Collins becomes the first woman to pilot a U.S. space shuttle

1996

Dolly the sheep is cloned in Scotland; she is the first mammal cloned from an adult cell

WORLD EVENTS

2003
Founds the Dolores
Huerta Foundation

2007
Continues to travel
throughout the
nation, speaking out
on issues that affect
farmworkers and
women

2000
Resigns from
the UFW

2005

2001
September 11 terrorist
attacks on the two World
Trade Center Towers in
New York City and on the
Pentagon in Washington,
D.C., leave thousands dead

2006
Within a day of
each other, two
women become
the first female
presidents of their
countries—Ellen
Johnson-Sirleaf in
Liberia and Michelle
Bachelet in Chile

2007
Former Vice
President Al Gore
and a United Nations
panel on climate
change win the
Nobel Peace Prize
for their efforts to
spread awareness
of global warming

DATE OF BIRTH: April 10, 1930

BIRTHPLACE: Dawson, New Mexico

FATHER: Juan Fernández

MOTHER: Alicia Chavez

EDUCATION: Attended University of the Pacific's Delta Community College, Stockton, California

FIRST SPOUSE: Ralph Head

DATE OF MARRIAGE: 1950

CHILDREN: Celeste (1951)
Lori (1952)

SECOND SPOUSE: Ventura Huerta

DATE OF MARRIAGE: 1955

CHILDREN: Fidel (1956)
Emilio (1957)
Vincent (1958)
Alicia (1959)
Angela (1963)

OTHER CHILDREN: with Richard Chavez (1929–)
Juanita (1970)
María Elena (1972)
Ricky (1973)
Camila (1976)

Further Reading

Chin-Lee, Cynthia. *Amelia to Zora: Twenty-Six Women Who Changed the World.* Watertown, Mass.: Charlesbridge Publishing, 2005.

Miller, Debra A. *Dolores Huerta: Labor Leader.* San Diego: Lucent Books, 2006.

Soto, Gary. *Jessie de la Cruz: Profile of a United Farm Worker.* New York: Persea Books, 2000.

Thompson, E.L. *Cesar Chavez, with profiles of Terence V. Powderly and Dolores Huerta.* Chicago: World Book, 2007.

Look for more Signature Lives
BOOKS ABOUT THIS ERA:

George Washington Carver: *Scientist, Inventor, and Teacher*

Cesar Chavez: *Heroic Crusader for Social Change*

Hillary Rodham Clinton: *First Lady and Senator*

Elizabeth Dole: *Public Servant and Senator*

Yo-Yo Ma: *Internationally Acclaimed Cellist*

Thurgood Marshall: *Civil Rights Lawyer and Supreme Court Justice*

Will Rogers: *Cowboy, Comedian, and Commentator*

Gloria Steinem: *Champion of Women's Rights*

Alice Walker: *Author and Social Activist*

Madam C.J. Walker: *Entrepreneur and Millionaire*

On the Web

For more information on this topic,
use FactHound.

1. Go to *www.facthound.com*
2. Type in this book ID: 0756534771
3. Click on the *Fetch It* button.

FactHound will find the best
Web sites for you.

Historic Sites

Forty Acres
30168 Garces Highway
Delano, CA 93216
661/725-9730
Site where the United Farm Workers
was founded

National Chavez Center
29700 Woodford-Tehachapi Road
Keene, CA 93531
661/823-6134
Museum and library honoring the work of
Cesar Chavez and other union organizers